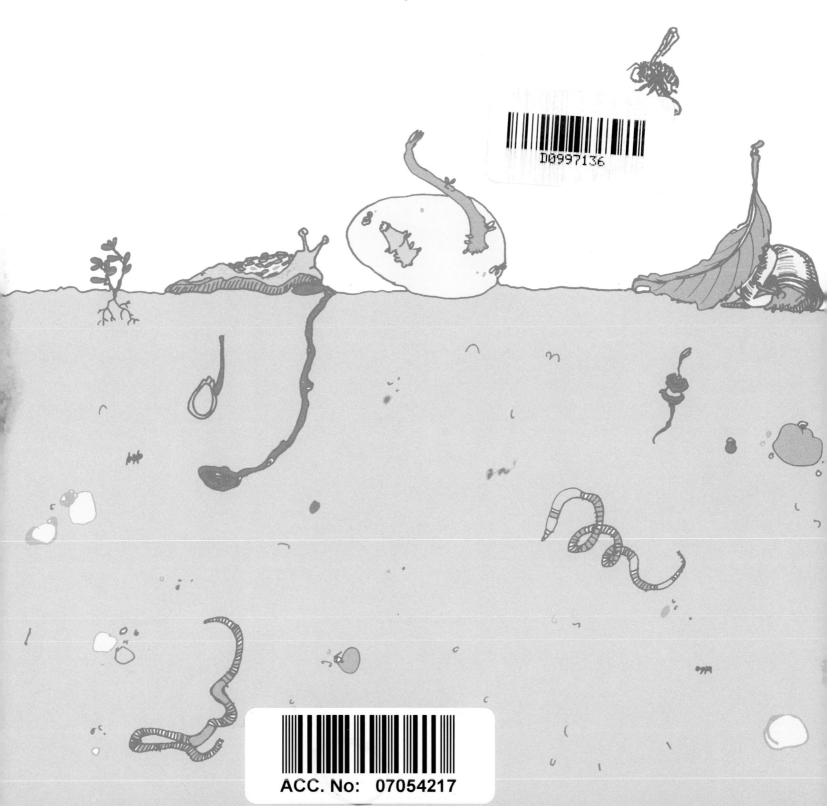

Plant, Sow, Make & Grow

MUD-TASTIC ACTIVITIES FOR BUDDING GARDENERS

Button
BOOKS

Esther Coombs

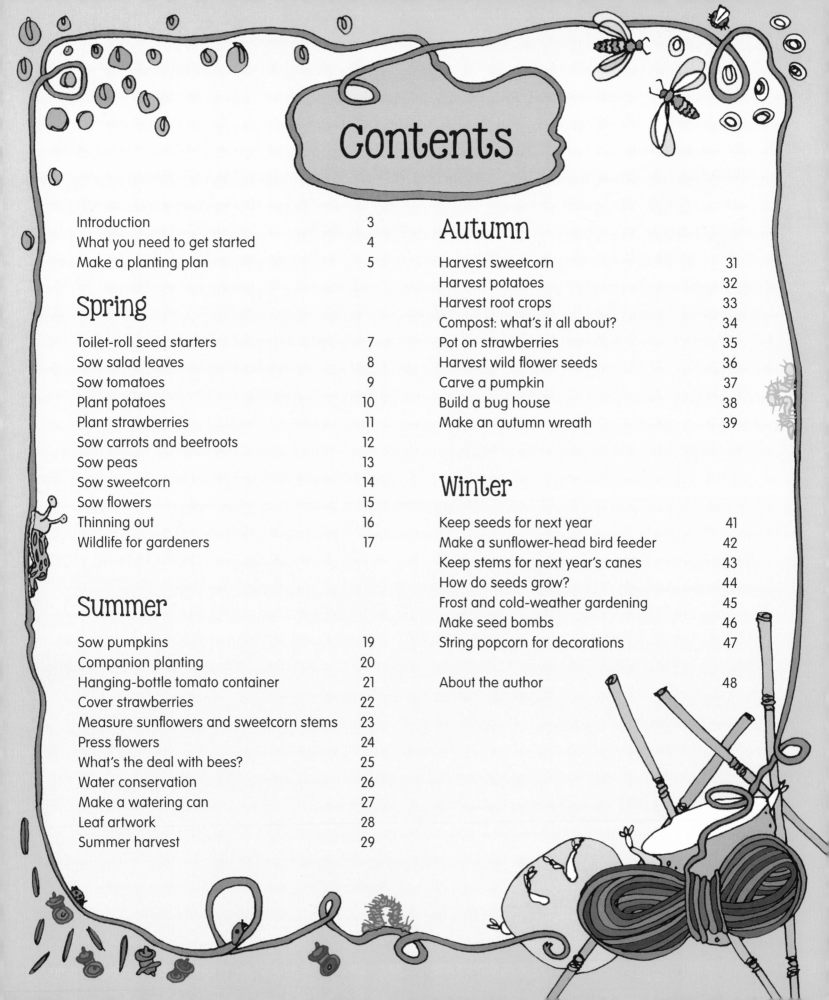

Contents

Introduction 3
What you need to get started 4
Make a planting plan 5

Spring

Toilet-roll seed starters 7
Sow salad leaves 8
Sow tomatoes 9
Plant potatoes 10
Plant strawberries 11
Sow carrots and beetroots 12
Sow peas 13
Sow sweetcorn 14
Sow flowers 15
Thinning out 16
Wildlife for gardeners 17

Summer

Sow pumpkins 19
Companion planting 20
Hanging-bottle tomato container 21
Cover strawberries 22
Measure sunflowers and sweetcorn stems 23
Press flowers 24
What's the deal with bees? 25
Water conservation 26
Make a watering can 27
Leaf artwork 28
Summer harvest 29

Autumn

Harvest sweetcorn 31
Harvest potatoes 32
Harvest root crops 33
Compost: what's it all about? 34
Pot on strawberries 35
Harvest wild flower seeds 36
Carve a pumpkin 37
Build a bug house 38
Make an autumn wreath 39

Winter

Keep seeds for next year 41
Make a sunflower-head bird feeder 42
Keep stems for next year's canes 43
How do seeds grow? 44
Frost and cold-weather gardening 45
Make seed bombs 46
String popcorn for decorations 47

About the author 48

Introduction

WHEN I STARTED GARDENING, I took a rather Russian roulette approach: I'd plant some seeds, water them, not worry too much, and then see what survived. It could be a bit hit or miss, but it was fun, not too time-consuming and something that I could enjoy with my daughter. Although in life I'm a bit of a perfectionist – and pretty impatient, too – I soon let go, and the result was a free-range approach to growing.

My daughter's new school had some potential gardening space in need of tender loving care (once a lot of rubbish had gone into a skip). After winning a small grant and with the help of another wonderful mum, I managed to get the 'garden' usable again and started a gardening club. When we began, I wasn't sure that I knew enough about gardening to pull it off, but plenty of enthusiasm and help made it work. Along the way I made small illustrated newsletters about our club and it was these that gave the idea for this book.

The pages that follow are full of everything I found useful when I started gardening with kids, divided into seasons and including crafting projects as well as growing ones. Children learn a huge amount from growing and you'll find that, once you've set the basics up, a lot of the learning comes naturally.

This book not only aims to show you how to grow food (a lovely, tasty money-saver), but also brings in maths, science and the arts along the way. You don't need much money or effort to make gardening work; you'll find lots of ideas here, whatever your available space and budget. Among many other things, you'll discover that, with small kids, worms are always a winner, and digging is a great way to tire them out (the kids, that is, not the worms).

I still run the gardening club, and hope to do so for a long time yet. Back at home, my veg patch and pots continue to grow, and I'm still pretty laid-back about how things go out there. You may find that just a few hours out gardening with your child makes you a convert. For me, it was picking peas straight from the plant and hearing my daughter describing them as 'garden sweeties' that made me a veg grower for life!

Thank you to Hatti, Annemarie and all the children at the Stelling Minnis Primary School Gardening Club. I learned a lot.

For Tinneke, who is my favourite gardener: let's grow peas that taste like sweeties and pumpkins bigger than grandad's every year!

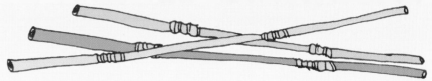

WHAT YOU NEED TO GET STARTED

Which tools and other bits do you really need? Here's a list of the basics. Some can be bought (car boot fairs often have great second-hand tools) and some you can make yourself.

Trowel or small shovel See page 38 for how to make your own.

Hand fork Used to break up hard surface soil or dig up larger weeds.

Watering can See page 27 for how to make one.

Gloves To protect you from spiky weeds and nettles.

String Any type; it doesn't have to be garden twine.

Compost Any general-purpose compost. Mixing bought compost half-and-half with garden soil makes it go much further. See page 34 for how to make your own compost.

Bubble wrap Great for protecting plants in winter; recycle what you can from parcels and packaging.

Netting Protects crops against birds. Buy a small roll or find some old net curtains in a charity shop.

Lolly sticks Make excellent seed markers.

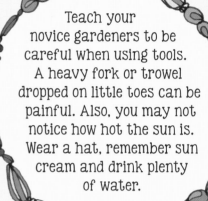

Teach your novice gardeners to be careful when using tools. A heavy fork or trowel dropped on little toes can be painful. Also, you may not notice how hot the sun is. Wear a hat, remember sun cream and drink plenty of water.

Kitchen utensils can be used in the garden. A metal spoon can help with potting up seedlings and a wooden spoon handle makes neat holes for seeds.

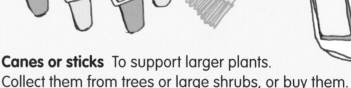

Canes or sticks To support larger plants. Collect them from trees or large shrubs, or buy them.

Containers Large, strong bags and plastic bottles can be used for crops you don't want to put in the ground. Smaller yogurt pots or juice cartons are great for seedlings.

MAKE A PLANTING PLAN

Before you start, it's helpful to have a plan. To make one, you need to look at how much space you have and what you want to try growing.

Start small, with one or two beds of about a metre square – it's easier to stay on top of weeding and watering and little gardeners will be able to reach the centre. If possible, choose a sunny spot as veg need plenty of light to grow.

Mark out the edge of the bed with a spade, dig up the turf and loosen the soil with a fork to about 30cm depth, bashing up any large lumps and then dig in some compost. Some gardeners may suggest more lengthy prep, but things have grown well for me with just these basic steps.

If you don't have open ground, you can make beds from large builders' sacks, filled with compost with a few drainage holes pierced around the base.

Divide the bed into clear areas for each type of crop. Check the size the plant is expected to reach and leave enough space for it. Remember, your seedlings won't stay tiny forever. Some crops, such as pumpkins, need lots of space.

Here are eight suggestions for first crops: easy fruit and veg that are simple to grow, reliable, and not too demanding!

Tomatoes
I've got a great plan for growing these out of the main bed. See page 21 for details.

Pumpkins   Potatoes   Strawberries

Beetroot

Sweetcorn*

Carrots

Peas

Nasturtiums

Sunflowers

Wild flowers

When you're buying seeds or baby plants look out for heirloom varieties, rather than hybrids. Find out why on page 41.

*Popping corn is a different variety of corn

Spring

TOILET-ROLL SEED STARTERS

These neat little pots get your seeds off to a good start. A cracking way to recycle: they're free, they're easy to make and you can simply put them straight into the ground. The cardboard degrades in the soil and so you won't disturb the roots of your baby plants.

> ## You will need
> - Tubes from the centres of loo rolls (each cardboard tube will make two pots)
> - Scissors
> - Compost or soil
> - Seeds

1 Press each tube flat. Then open it out and flatten it across the opposite way. When open, it should have four corners, making a square shape.

2 Cut upwards at each corner of the square with scissors, approximately 2cm, to create four flaps.

3 Fold each flap in and out again, making a crease at the base.

4 Fold the flaps into the centre to make the base of the pot. Tuck one side of the final flap under the edge of the first flap to secure.

5 Fill each pot with compost, plant each with a seed or seeds, and water lightly. The pots aren't watertight, so they need to stand on a tray. You can put a rubber band around a few of them to keep them steady.

Small seeds can be scattered over the top of the soil with just a dusting of compost over them. Larger seeds, such as peas and beans, should be planted about 2cm deep, then covered over with compost. Be careful not to sow seeds too deep.

SOW SALAD LEAVES

Salad leaves are incredibly easy and quick to grow. To harvest, you cut the leaves off a couple of centimetres from the ground, and more leaves will quickly grow back. That's why they're called a cut-and-come-again crop.

1 Fill the container with compost or loosen and level the soil where you want to plant.

2 Make a shallow groove in the soil of the container or ground by running your finger in a line where you want to sow.

3 Scatter seeds thinly into the groove (each seed may grow several salad leaves, so you don't need to use too many).

4 About a week later, the seeds should have sprouted. Once the leaves are big enough, cut them around 2cm above the ground.

Protect salad leaves from extremes of temperature: they don't like frost and will wilt in very hot weather. Sow a second container next week, and a third the week after for a regular supply. You can also put a tiny quantity of compost into eggshells and sow cress in them, an old-school classic.

You will need
• A container (or prepared soil if you're planting into the ground)
• Soil or compost
• Seeds for salad greens

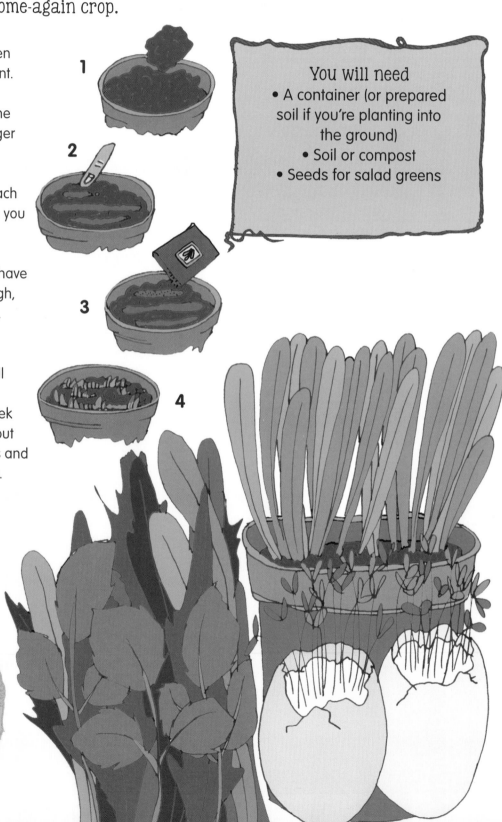

These are some of the most nutritious greens you'll ever eat: from plot to plate, with no nasty chemicals. The seeds are cheap and there are hundreds in each packet.

SOW TOMATOES

Even kids who claim to be tomato-haters scoff handfuls of these small, round, warm mouthfuls of exploding yumminess, so tomatoes should certainly go on your growing list.

What's the downside?
Tomatoes are needy. They like about six hours of sunshine a day, moist soil, regular feeds, sturdy supports and shelter from the wind. They can be prone to diseases, and you can't recycle the soil they're grown in.

The solution is to grow them in containers. You can move the pots to shelter, they are easier to water and need less soil. They can also be kept separate from other plants to avoid the spread of disease. Cherry tomatoes are perfect for pots. They are a small bush variety that bear lots of fruit and don't need much support. Problem solved; let's grow!

You will need
- Cherry tomato seeds
- Toilet-roll starter pots
- Compost
- Small pots with holes in the bottom

1 Plant the seeds into toilet-roll starter pots (see page 7) filled with compost. Leave them on a sunny windowsill to germinate.

2 When the seedlings start to outgrow the pots, move them on into slightly larger ones.

3 Pop them outside during the day to harden them up before potting up in early summer (see page 21).

If you don't have a sunny spot indoors, a plastic bag put over the pots will speed things up.

When you're potting on, old yogurt pots with holes pierced in the base work well.

9

PLANT POTATOES

Potatoes are so simple to grow. When an old potato produces little shoots, it's ready to start making a new plant. Grab some that have started to sprout, pop them into an empty egg box with sprouts facing upwards and place by a window to chit.

You will need
- A few sprouting potatoes (or seed potatoes)
- Empty egg boxes
- Container or strong bag with drainage holes and compost (optional)
- Spade

1 Your potatoes are ready to plant when the shoots are several centimetres long. They can go into your veg patch, a plastic tub, a sack or a strong carrier bag.

2 If you're planting in a bag or container, fill it to about a third full of compost and soil mixed together. Put the potatoes on top, and cover with more compost. Water. If you're planting in the ground, dig a trench about 30cm deep. Keep the soil you've dug out heaped up along one side, place your potatoes along the bottom, and cover them with a spadeful or so of soil, then water.

3 When green shoots have grown between 10cm and 15cm high, cover them with soil, leaving a couple of centimetres showing (this is called 'hilling up'). It hides the potatoes from the light (which would make them go green) and increases the crop. Keep covering up the shoots every time they get to 15cm high.

4 If you're growing in a container, leave the plants to grow when the soil reaches the top. If you're growing in the ground, use the soil piled up next to the trench. When that's used, dig soil from the ground to either side of the potato row to make little hills over the plants.

'Chitting' describes the process of an old potato growing shoots.

Disease-resistant 'seed' potatoes for early and late in the growing season may give you more reliable results. However, I've never bothered; I just chit leftover potatoes from the kitchen.

5 When the hill is 30cm high, leave the potato plants to grow. Now all they need is regular watering.

PLANT STRAWBERRIES

Strawberries are so delicious and easy to grow that they often entice children into the garden. My own patch started small but grows bigger every year and we have had a bowl of them on the table every day through the fruiting season. Amazing!

Although strawberries can be grown from seed, it can be tricky to get them going. It's easy and affordable to buy a few small plants from a garden centre instead. Once they are growing, you'll never need to buy them again, so they are a good investment. Strawberries are happy in the ground or in a container. Window boxes or hanging baskets are ideal. Keep an eye on them – birds like the fruit almost as much as kids do.

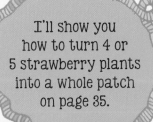

I'll show you how to turn 4 or 5 strawberry plants into a whole patch on page 35.

Wild strawberries are smaller than 'tame' (ordinary) ones. They have a stronger and slightly sour flavour, but are still delicious. The plants are also smaller than their larger cousins, so they're a good choice if you don't have much space.

Wild strawberry

Standard strawberry

Pop your plants into the soil at the depth shown opposite, and leave them to get on with it. They need a sunny spot and plenty of water when it's warm.

Too deep

Just right

Too shallow

11

SOW CARROTS AND BEETROOT

These are veggie-patch classics and it's easy to see why: they don't need pollinating, they're reliable croppers, they're low maintenance (apart from keeping pests away) and they're a wonderful surprise when you pull them up. What's not to love?

If you have a small garden, or no garden at all, use containers, such as deep buckets, barrels or large builders' sacks.

1 Smooth the soil in the container or the veg patch to get a flattish surface. If you're growing in containers, you may opt for a container each for beetroot and carrot.

2 Using your finger or the point of a trowel, draw two lines in the soil, marking rows for the seeds to drop into – one for beetroot, one for carrots. Or, mark a row or small circle in each container.

3 Seed packets tell you how close to plant seeds but I generally ignore them. Hold a heap of seeds in one hand, pinch up a few with the fingers of the other, then sprinkle them along the row, close to the soil.

4 When you've planted a row of each crop, cover the seeds with a little soil. Water lightly.

Will you find carrots in the beetroot row? Probably! But carrots and beetroot have very different leaves so you can have fun working out which is which as they grow.

Beetroot has been eaten in space! In 1975, Russian astronauts cooked up a big meal of borscht (beetroot soup) for their American co-workers – with zero gravity.

SOW PEAS

'They are like garden sweeties', said my daughter... I grow peas every year, and she eats them shelled, straight from the plant. They are delicious.

Peas are easy to grow from seed, and if, after your first crop, you store some to use as seed next year, you won't ever need to buy more. (see page 41.) You can start peas off inside on your windowsill in pots (see page 7), or sow them directly into your veggie patch or container.

To sow peas, pop a seed into a starter pot or, if you're putting them direct in the ground, in a row, planted around 2cm deep, with about 15–30cm space between each seed.

There's no rush to plant them outside, as peas don't like it to be too cold or damp, so wait until the last frost is over and spring is warming up. This is often during April; but a little later won't hurt.

They are climbers so they'll need support. Good-sized sticks or branches will do the job if you don't want to buy canes. Once planted, you can watch them grow, flower and produce peas. Easy!

Did you know that Native Americans used to grow climbing crops, like beans and peas, next to sweetcorn so that the climbers could use the stalks as supports to grow up? Genius! This is called companion planting, find out more on page 20.

13

SOW SWEETCORN

Sweetcorn is good fun to grow: children love the huge plants, which grow taller than they are, and fresh corn on the cob is popular with pretty much everyone, young or old. Eaten straight from the plant, it's delicious.

Sweetcorn isn't keen on the cold, so wait to sow it when the weather has warmed up in late spring. Remember just how big these plants will grow. No sprinkling this time. Mark out where to make holes by putting your foot in between to measure out roughly (a great chance to get muddy) before making a hole for the next seed.

When you grow sweetcorn, you get to see its whole life cycle. Starting with the seed, you plant it, harvest the crop, eat some and save a bit to plant the next year… and so on.

There are two types of corn to try. First, there's classic sweetcorn, which is bright yellow (and delicious with a blob of butter) and then there's popping corn, which, as you'd guess from the name, is the sort you make popcorn with. Grow both if you can: producing a bowl of your very own popcorn (which you can dry to store over winter) is about as close to magic as you can get when it comes to growing veg.

Sweetcorn is wind-pollinated, and needs to be close to other plants. Sow several plants in a block, rather than a row, to ensure success.

Popping corn often comes in colours other than the classic yellow, so it's easy to tell the difference between the two types.

You can't pop regular sweetcorn; you need to buy special popcorn seed instead.

14

SOW FLOWERS

It's wonderful to be able to eat what you grow, but a plot without flowers will struggle to attract bees and other pollinators, which many fruit and veg need.

Sowing wild flowers, nasturtiums or sunflowers among your other crops solves the problem. They're great for bees, and they either self-seed or have seeds you can easily harvest to sow again next year.

If you're super-organized and are already thinking ahead to next year, plant some crocus bulbs in the early autumn. They offer pollinators a great source of food in early spring when it's scarce.

Sunflowers not only look wonderful but you can use them instead of canes to support climbing crops such as peas, or use the seeds as bird food – birds love them!

Nasturtiums are edible as well as colourful. The wide petals aren't just excellent landing pads for insects: you can eat them, too. They taste peppery and look great on salads.

Wild flowers are brilliant for very young gardeners. They can be bought in mixed packets and scattered where you'd like them to grow. Sprinkle a little compost on top, water and you've got a colourful, insect-friendly patch.

Turn to page 42 to learn how to use a sunflower to make a simple bird feeder.

15

THINNING OUT

Keep a watch on the little seedling leaves when they first come up. If the seed was sown a bit unevenly, the result will be a clump of seedlings growing too close together. All you need to do is gently pinch a few out, giving the rest more space to grow bigger.

Thinning out is more fun than it sounds, and when you've finished, it's satisfying to know that though you'll have fewer vegetables when it comes to harvest time, they'll be much larger and stronger.

Small seedlings often don't like to be moved (it damages their roots), so discard the ones you pull up rather than replanting them – moving them somewhere else is unlikely to get you great results. If you end up with any large gaps, re-sow to fill them.

Keep an eye out for pests such as pigeons or other bigger birds, who love the tiny shoots to eat. You can net your veg to protect it, as you do strawberries, or use home-made scarers to deter birds (see page 22). But don't worry – usually enough seedlings make it through to adulthood to give you a successful crop.

Do you know why most of the carrots we grow are orange? Long ago, when the Dutch ruler was William of Orange, local growers cultivated orange carrots as a tribute to him. Other colours of carrot (white, yellow and purple) fell out of popularity. You can still grow other colours, look out for seeds in more exotic shades!

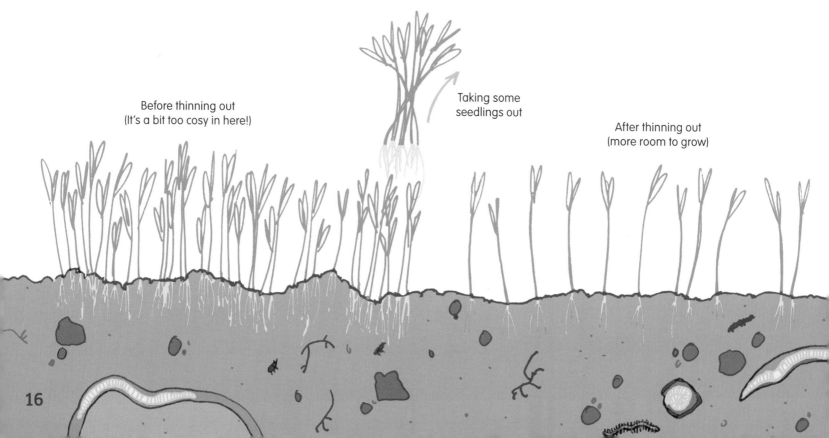

Before thinning out
(It's a bit too cosy in here!)

Taking some seedlings out

After thinning out
(more room to grow)

WILDLIFE FOR GARDENERS

The good-to-know wildlife list for your garden.

The good:

Ladybirds They're not only fun to spot and spotty to count, but they also eat aphids. Ladybirds love nasturtiums, which are bright, full of nectar and attract plenty of aphids for them to eat!

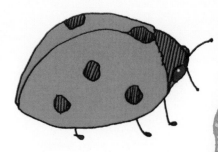

Ants can be baddies disguised as goodies. It can look as if ants are eating aphids but they are actually aphid farmers. They love the sugary liquid aphids excrete and when you see them nearby, they're milking them for a tasty snack. Clever ants!

Frogs These guys are brilliant helpers; they won't eat the veggies but will eat slugs, snails and caterpillars. If you can, encourage them with a mini pond: it'll be worth it.

The bad:

Aphids (aka greenfly) Aphids multiply so quickly they can suck your crops dry. You can use natural and organic pesticides, but the best answer is a population of ladybirds to eat them!

Bees They're expert pollinators, and plenty of bees is a sure-fire sign of a happy garden. They particularly love a wild flower meadow (see page 25 for more).

If you've got masses of aphids and not enough predators, try spraying with a mix of washing-up liquid diluted with water. It really works!

Slugs Mowing down seedlings and making holes in veg, they can be hard to beat, so be sure to encourage the natural slug eaters – birds, frogs and hedgehogs.

Caterpillars They love to munch leaves; eating everything but the stems! Frogs and birds eat them so encourage birds to hang around by feeding them.

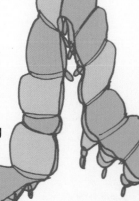

Summer

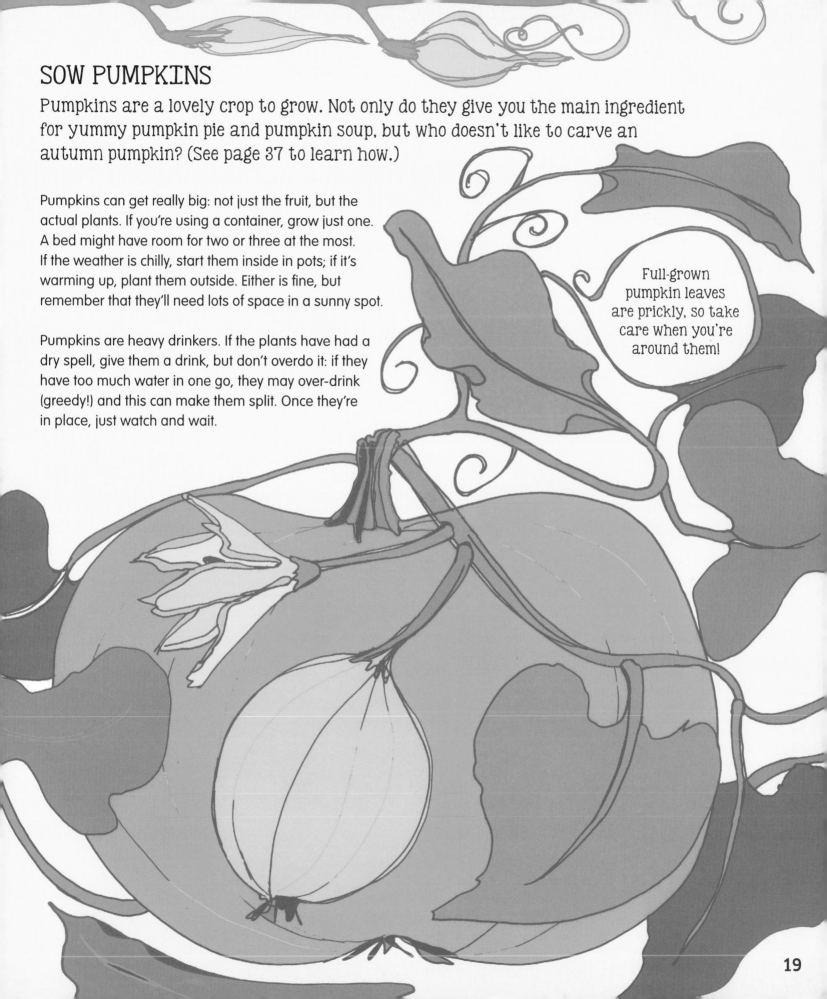

SOW PUMPKINS

Pumpkins are a lovely crop to grow. Not only do they give you the main ingredient for yummy pumpkin pie and pumpkin soup, but who doesn't like to carve an autumn pumpkin? (See page 37 to learn how.)

Pumpkins can get really big: not just the fruit, but the actual plants. If you're using a container, grow just one. A bed might have room for two or three at the most. If the weather is chilly, start them inside in pots; if it's warming up, plant them outside. Either is fine, but remember that they'll need lots of space in a sunny spot.

Pumpkins are heavy drinkers. If the plants have had a dry spell, give them a drink, but don't overdo it: if they have too much water in one go, they may over-drink (greedy!) and this can make them split. Once they're in place, just watch and wait.

Full-grown pumpkin leaves are prickly, so take care when you're around them!

COMPANION PLANTING

This means putting different plants that can be mutually helpful close to one another in the veg patch and it has been going on for hundreds, or even thousands, of years.

Early gardeners soon learned that tall, strong stalks (like those of corn) would give extra support for climbers (such as peas or beans). If you want to try this combination for yourself, remember to plant your sweetcorn or sunflowers first, so that they're big and strong enough to support the peas by the time they have grown tall enough to cling on.

Companion planting can also help you fend off nasty pests! Peas hate aphids, and aphids love nasturtiums, so if you grow the two close together, the nasturtiums will attract the aphids away from your pea crop. As an added bonus, ladybirds also love the vibrant colours and the deep nectar stocks of nasturtiums. Nothing makes a ladybird happier than a feast of aphids!

A traditional Native American plant combination is sweetcorn, beans and squash (known as 'the Three Sisters'). The corn grows tall to support the beans, the beans give nitrogen to the soil and the squash covers the ground with its prickly leaves to see off predators and keep the soil moist.

HANGING-BOTTLE TOMATO CONTAINER

When your tomato seedlings are around 10cm tall with their little roots poking out of the bottoms of their pots, they're ready to be treated as adult plants and be potted on. This clever hanging-bottle planter is an ideal way to grow your tomatoes.

Cherry tomatoes, or any other small bush variety, will grow happily planted in hanging baskets, or upside down in hanging bottles. Gravity means that the branches don't need extra support, the plant catches the maximum amount of sun and hanging means they aren't taking up ground space.

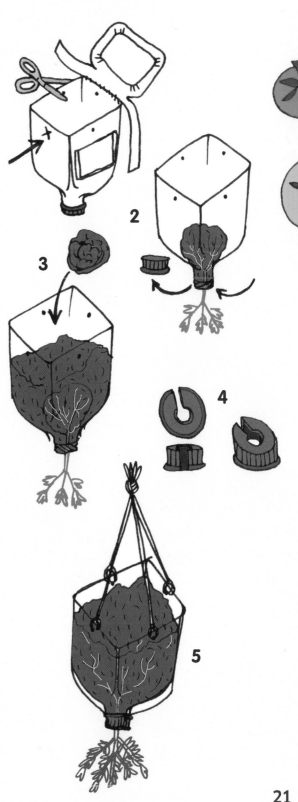

You will need
- A large, square plastic bottle
- Scissors
- String
- Compost
- Tomato plant

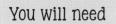

Tomatoes that don't ripen can be made into green tomato chutney. Yum!

Did you know that tomatoes are actually a fruit, not a vegetable?

1 Cut the base off the bottle and use scissors to make a hole in the centre of each side, about 2cm down from the cut edge.

2 Unscrew the bottle top. Take the tomato plant out of its pot and feed the roots through the mouth of the bottle so they are inside.

3 Holding the plant in place, turn the bottle upside down and fill it with compost, patting it down around the roots.

4 Use the scissors to cut a key-shaped hole out of the bottle top.

5 With the bottle upside down, carefully slide the top back in place, with the tomato stem fitting through the hole, and screw it back on. Thread a double length of string through each of the four holes in the sides and tie them together. Now hang your container up!

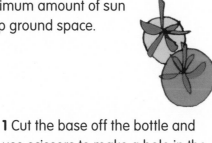

COVER STRAWBERRIES

If your strawberry plants are growing in a container or the veg patch and you can see tiny white strawberries beginning to grow, they now need to be protected.

The birds will have noticed them too, so your next mission is to cover the fruit to stop it from being eaten. The best thing to use is netting. If the fruit is growing in a container, you can just throw a net over it, but if the plants are in the ground, the pesky birds may still find their way through, so the best answer is to build a little frame around them, and drape the netting over that.

You will need
- Netting (from a garden centre, or find old net curtains at a charity shop)
- 8 canes or sticks
- String
- Bricks or heavy stones

Did you know that strawberries are the only fruit to carry their seeds on the outside?

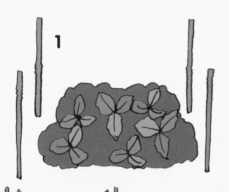

1 Push a cane into the ground at each corner of the strawberry patch.

2 Line up the remaining four canes horizontally across the tops of the corner stakes and bind them around with string to create a frame (an extra pair of hands will help for this job).

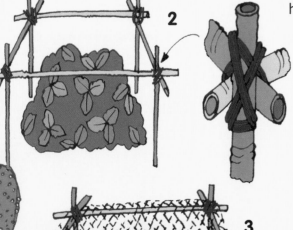

3 When the frame is secure, arrange the net over the top and down the sides. Weigh down the edges on the ground with bricks or heavy stones.

Make bird scarers by taping strips of foil-lined crisp packets to one end of a cane. The rustle of them blowing in the wind will frighten the birds away.

Get the kids to spot the birds that come visiting with these fun binoculars. Glue two toilet-roll centres together, pierce a hole at each side with a pencil point, thread string through and tie a knot on the inside.

MEASURE SUNFLOWERS AND SWEETCORN STEMS

Sunflowers and sweetcorn are not only good crops - easy to grow, yummy to eat (with sweetcorn, the cobs; with sunflowers, the seeds) - but they also grow very tall, super tall.

Everyone loves charting their progress as they grow. Try measuring them alongside the kids every week: snap a picture of your child or children standing next to the plant and see who grows fastest! You could even set up a child/sunflower or sweetcorn race.

If you don't have much room, you can find dwarf varieties of both sunflowers and sweetcorn. They will take up much less space in your plot.

Did you know sunflowers are so-called because their faces turn towards the sun as it moves across the sky?

Sweetcorn is grown on every continent in the world except Antarctica. An ear of corn always has an even number of rows, base to tip.

The tallest corn plant on record reached an incredible 13.7 metres.

The tallest sunflower reached 9.17 metres.

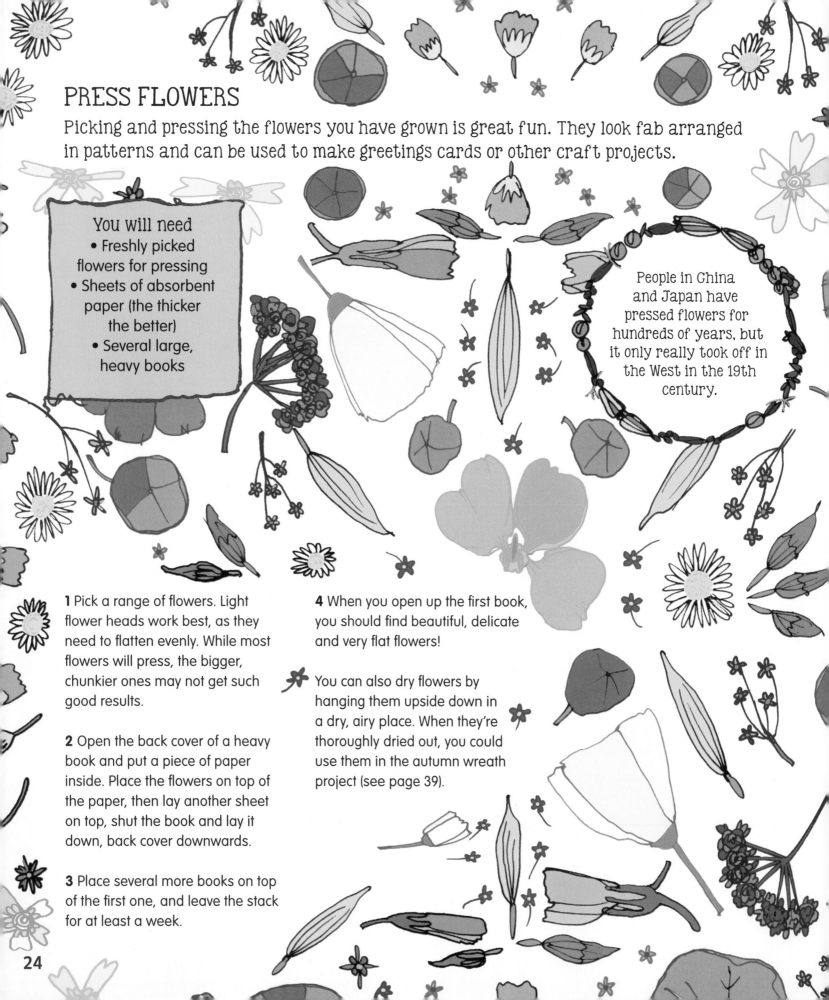

PRESS FLOWERS

Picking and pressing the flowers you have grown is great fun. They look fab arranged in patterns and can be used to make greetings cards or other craft projects.

You will need
- Freshly picked flowers for pressing
- Sheets of absorbent paper (the thicker the better)
- Several large, heavy books

People in China and Japan have pressed flowers for hundreds of years, but it only really took off in the West in the 19th century.

1 Pick a range of flowers. Light flower heads work best, as they need to flatten evenly. While most flowers will press, the bigger, chunkier ones may not get such good results.

2 Open the back cover of a heavy book and put a piece of paper inside. Place the flowers on top of the paper, then lay another sheet on top, shut the book and lay it down, back cover downwards.

3 Place several more books on top of the first one, and leave the stack for at least a week.

4 When you open up the first book, you should find beautiful, delicate and very flat flowers!

You can also dry flowers by hanging them upside down in a dry, airy place. When they're thoroughly dried out, you could use them in the autumn wreath project (see page 39).

WHAT'S THE DEAL WITH BEES?

As you probably already know, for gardeners (well, for everyone really) bees are kind of a big deal. They are one of the most important pollinators and the majority of plants need their help to reproduce and grow fruit.

Not only are bees crucial, but they're also under threat: their numbers are dropping fast. So what are the best ways to encourage them into your garden to help to pollinate your fruit and vegetables?

The most useful thing that you can do is to plant flowers that are full of the energy-rich nectar that bees crave (and don't be too hasty to pull out dandelions or buttercups – bees love them).

A few of the best bee-friendly flowers:

Crocuses These bulbs are small but rich in nectar – plus they grow early in spring, at a time when bees desperately need food.

Lavender A real crowd-pleaser for both bees and people. Lots of small flowers grow close together so the bees can hop from one tiny bloom to the next, and you'll love the smell, too.

Sunflowers These are huge pollen-laden targets for bees – bright, packed full of tiny flowers and yellow enough to look like honey itself! Often found in family gardens during the summer, they are bee heaven.

Honeybees live in hives, but many other bee species are solitary, nesting in the ground or over-wintering in hollow stems or branches. Solitary bees will appreciate a custom-made house (see page 38).

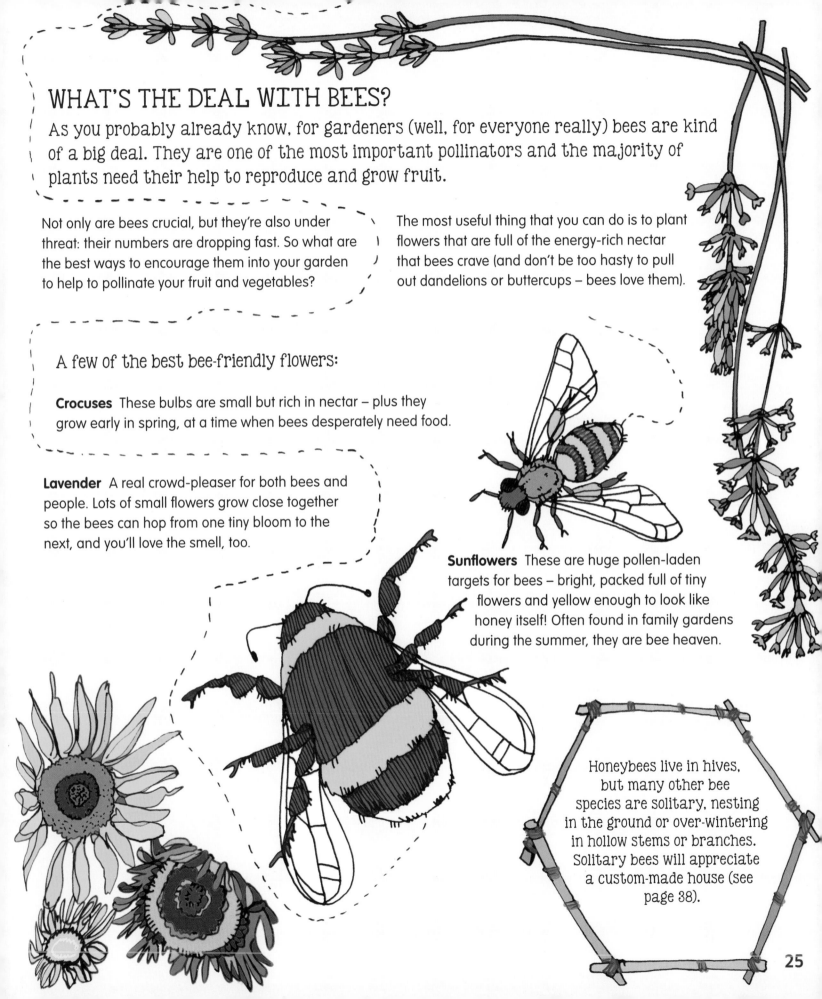

25

WATER CONSERVATION

In warmer, drier weather, most gardeners do their best to save water. Here are some top tips to bear in mind.

- Water early or late in the day, to avoid water evaporating in the heat before it does any good.
- A good soak that gets to the roots is best.
- Mulching or laying down grass cuttings helps to reduce evaporation (and keeps weeds down).
- If you have room, invest in a water butt.
- Crops that will do well in a dry summer include rhubarb, carrots, beetroot, parsnips and tomatoes. Avoid leafy greens, such as salad leaves, which won't cope so well with drought.

Kate Sessions

Back in the 1890s, a person who knew how to deal with hot weather was an American gardener called Kate Sessions. She created a lush park in San Diego, California, where people had thought it was too dry for anything to grow.

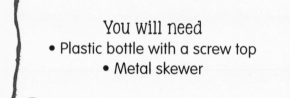

You will need
- Plastic bottle with a screw top
- Metal skewer

1 Make a row of small holes around the bottom of the bottle using a skewer.

2 Bury the bottle next to a plant you want to water, as far down as the roots spread. Leave the top of the bottle above ground.

3 Fill the bottle with water, then replace the lid. The bottle will slowly release water direct to the roots.

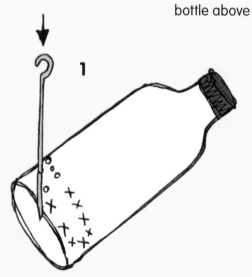

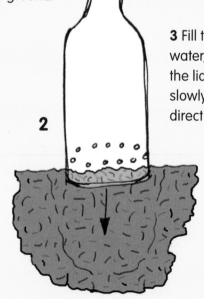

MAKE A WATERING CAN

Here's how to make a DIY watering can. It's simple to do and it's perfect for little hands to use. This could work with all kinds of cartons or bottles.

You will need
- Plastic bottle with a handle and screw top
- Push pin
- Sharp pencil

1 Remove the cap from the bottle and use the push pin to make between 15 and 20 holes in it.

2 Use the point of the pencil to push through and enlarge the holes.

3 Use the push pin to make a hole in the handle, and enlarge it using the pencil point. It should be slightly bigger than the ones in the cap. (This hole lets air back into the bottle and helps a steady stream of water to come out of the cap holes.)

4 Fill the bottle with water and replace the cap. You're now ready to get watering.

LEAF ARTWORK

Long, sunny summer days spent outside call for some extra ideas for ways to keep children busy and entertained. Painting and printing with leaves is the perfect easy activity.

Summer is an exciting time. Your plants will be maturing fast and some of the crops will already be ripening. After you've watered, weeded and looked for pests, why not spend a bit of time crafting with leaves? Pick the leaves from your largest, healthiest plants; they won't miss them. Then add a little paint and you're set: you can paint or print, whichever you and the kids prefer.

You will need
- Several kinds of large leaves
- Several colours of poster or acrylic paint (don't use watercolour)
- Paintbrushes
- Rolling pin
- Paper

Painting leaves
You can paint all kinds of creatures on leaves, but why not begin with a simple ladybird?

1 Paint a red oval that takes up most of the leaf.

2 Paint a small curved section in black over one end of the red oval.

3 Paint a black line down the middle of the oval, then add some black spots on either side.

4 Add six black legs and two little eyes in any other colour on the black section.

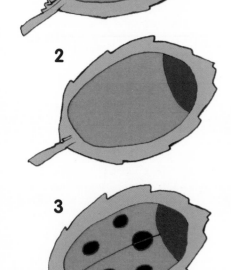

Printing with leaves
When you've printed a few single leaves, try making patterns with different colours and leaf shapes on large sheets of paper.

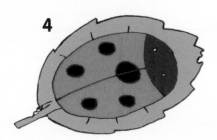

1 Brush a thin layer of paint over the whole underside of a leaf.

2 Place the leaf paint-side down on a piece of paper. Roll carefully over it with the rolling pin.

3 Gently peel the leaf off the paper, taking care not to smudge the print as you lift it.

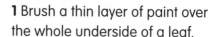

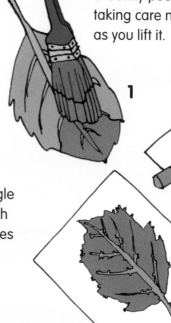

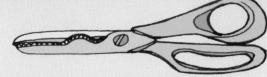

SUMMER HARVEST

You should be starting to see the results of your hard work, so here are some tips on harvesting (I'll cover sweetcorn, root crops, pumpkins and potatoes in the Autumn chapter).

Strawberries One of the earliest plants to crop. It's tempting to pick them when they're still pink but they taste best when the whole fruit is red.

Tomatoes It can feel slow for them to ripen, but once you see the first tomato flush with orange, you'll soon find the whole crop is ripe. If they don't all ripen, you can still make yummy chutney with green tomatoes.

Peas I like eating peas straight off the plant when they're still small, very green and sweet. But you can leave them to reach full size, when the pods are fat and you can see the rounded peas inside. Shell and cook them straight away once picked.

Sunflowers When a sunflower has flowered and its petals have wilted, cut down both stem and flower head, cut the head from the stem and take it inside to dry out. See pages 41–43 for information on ways to use them.

Nasturtiums You may have planted them for colour, or to attract aphids, but nasturtiums also make a good addition to salads. Pick and wash the petals: they look lovely and have an interesting, spicy flavour.

Salad leaves You've probably been eating these for some time already, but remember that cut-and-come-again salad can be cut a couple of centimetres from the ground and the plants will grow back to give you more salad one or two weeks later.

Early potatoes and root crops If you have grown early potatoes or managed to sow root veg such as carrots and beetroots very early you may already be harvesting them. See pages 32–33 for more information.

What to do with a glut

When all of one sort of fruit or veg ripens at once, so you have more than you can eat, it's known as having a 'glut'. So what should you do? There are lots of ways to turn a glut to your advantage.

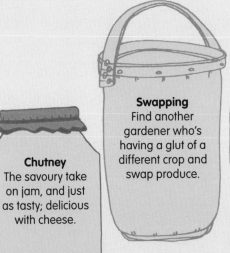

Pickling Fruit and veg can be preserved in jars with vinegar and herbs, where they will keep for a long time.

Freezing Pick and wash your crop, pop it in a bag or on a tray, and get it into the freezer as soon as possible.

Jam This is a favourite for dealing with a strawberry glut in my house, and good for most fruit.

Chutney The savoury take on jam, and just as tasty; delicious with cheese.

Swapping Find another gardener who's having a glut of a different crop and swap produce.

Giving away Family and friends will love your spare crops. Call around your local food bank or homeless shelter as many of them are grateful for fresh produce.

29

Autumn

HARVEST SWEETCORN

By early autumn, your sweetcorn stalks may have grown taller than you! You'll be able to see big ears of corn developing on them; peel back some of the leaves that grow tightly around them and have a peek to find out when they'll be ripe.

How do you know when to harvest? You need to be on 'silk watch'. These are the wispy threads that grow out of the top of a corn ear, and when the ear is fertilized and as big as it's going to grow, the silks turn brown. Peel back a leaf and press a kernel with your fingernail, if the cob is ripe, a milky liquid will come out, but if the liquid is clear, it's not ready yet.

Corn on the cob tastes sweetest cooked and eaten immediately because as soon as it's picked the sugars inside start turning to starch - so you'll never have a more delicious cob than one grown at home!

Too early   Almost ready   Pick me soon

When you know a cob is ready, pick it, take the leaves and silk off, and cook it straight away. It makes a very easy supper: boil a pan of water, pop the trimmed cobs in, boil for 5 minutes, drain and serve with plenty of butter.

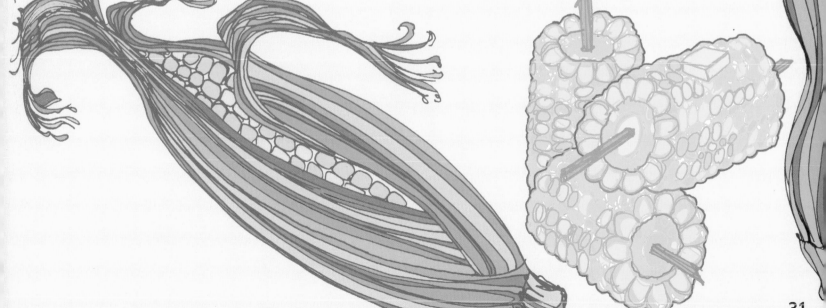

HARVEST POTATOES

When a potato plant's leaves are fully grown, the plant will flower, then wilt and look a bit sad. It's time for the good bit: digging for buried treasure.

After the hard work of hilling up, make the most of this wonderful moment. Have a bucket, ruler, paper and pencil to hand so that you can record how many potatoes you dig up, and how big your largest one grew.

Bend the foliage to one side and gently dig around the roots with a fork (be careful not to spear the potatoes). Lift the soil and watch as the crop comes to light. Move the earth carefully so you don't miss any.

If you grew your potatoes in containers, the easiest way to harvest them is to turn the container out on to a tarp or newspaper, then pick the potatoes out of the soil.

Potatoes can be left in the ground for a while before harvesting, even after the parent plant has wilted: they won't come to any harm.

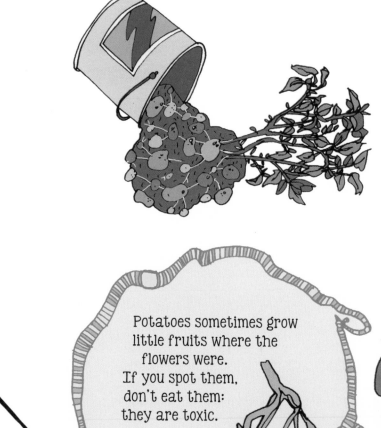

Spuds without scratches or bruises can be stored in a paper bag or sack for some time. Potatoes with blemishes are still fine to eat, but won't store well.

Green potatoes should be discarded, as they can be toxic. If any are only partly green, you need to cut all traces of green off before eating. Green potatoes have been exposed to light, probably growing too close to the soil surface, or needed more hilling up.

Potatoes sometimes grow little fruits where the flowers were. If you spot them, don't eat them: they are toxic.

HARVEST ROOT CROPS

Root crops are perfect for children to harvest. When the leaves on top have grown bushy and you can see the tops just breaking through, they're ready. Just grab the leaves firmly and pull!

If your carrots or beetroots prove tough to pull up, you can loosen the soil around them a little with a fork. Depending on when you sowed them, they may be ready to harvest any time from summer to late autumn. Cook them as soon as you can; the flavour is a hundred times better when they're fresh.

If you find yourself with a glut of beetroots or carrots, you can juice or pickle them but you can also leave them in the ground, provided it's not waterlogged, for some time, then pull them up as you need them.

Beetroots are messy to prepare. I use my grandmother's technique: wash them, cut the leaves off, then boil them whole. When cooked, turn the heat off. Once cool, rub the outer skin off into the pan. It's not completely mess-free, but it does confine it to the pan!

Carrots can grow into very odd shapes. These can be very entertaining and are perfectly edible. Twisty carrots are great!

COMPOST: WHAT'S IT ALL ABOUT?

Composting was a bit of a mystery to me until I inherited someone else's compost heap. Then, when I realized how easy it is to make rich compost, and how great it is for my veg patch, I kept it up and I'd encourage you to compost, too.

Composting can seem tricky. So much information can be confusing but don't be put off by all the rules and guidelines. Remember, you'll save money and trips to the garden centre and making your own is good for the environment – you'll be diverting waste from landfill. It's an all-round winner.

You can speed up composting by keeping the bin in a sunny, warm site, and chopping up items into small pieces.

You will need
• Plastic bin with a lid (the larger it is, the more compost you'll make)
• Drill
• Hacksaw

Warning!

If a heap gets too hot it can kill the beneficial bacteria and even combust. Stir and turn it often. If it's very hot in the centre, rake into smaller heaps and soak with water.

1 Use the drill to make rows of holes around the bin (to allow air to circulate). Cut the base off the bin with a hacksaw, so that it can sit directly on the ground (this will help with drainage).

2 Put the bin in a convenient corner, where it can sit directly on the soil, won't need to be moved but is easily accessible for emptying waste.

3 Now you're ready to start. What should you put in it? Try to balance it with about half garden waste, such as leaves, hedge and grass cuttings, and half kitchen scraps. Think of your bin as vegan – you shouldn't compost bones, meat scraps or dairy. Compost also finds too much citrus indigestible.

Kids might enjoy sorting the kitchen scraps and putting the right ones in the compost. Not much can go wrong, and it's fun chucking stuff into the bin.

Compost takes about a year to rot down and be ready: if you start now, next year you'll have a great free addition for your vegetable patch, ready for next autumn.

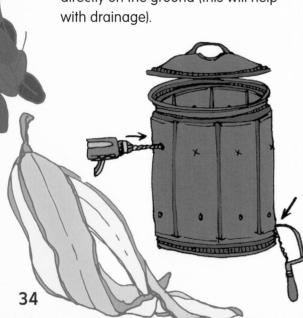

POT ON STRAWBERRIES

Now that you've enjoyed plenty of home-grown strawberries, you'll be pleased to learn that there's a cheap and easy way to multiply your plants for an even larger crop next year.

Every strawberry plant throws out runners. What does this mean? Well, the plant sends out little stems that initially look as though they're going to turn into leaves, but which instead, over time, grow away from the plant, then send down roots below and grow leaves on top. If it finds a patch of soil nearby where it can take root, then every runner can become a brand-new plant.

If you end up with too many baby plants, they make great gifts for friends.

Strawberry plants only fruit well for three years, so pot on runners so that you have young stock to replace the older plants as they stop cropping.

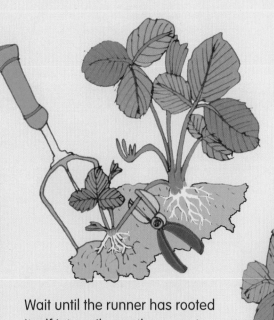

Mother plant

Daughter plant

Runner

Wait until the runner has rooted itself into soil near the parent plant, then dig it up, cutting the stem that attaches it. Put it into a pot with a little compost and leave to grow.

If you're growing in pots, let the runners grow until you see small roots starting to sprout. Place them on to the surface of a smaller pot nearby. Once they take root, cut them off and pot them up. If left, the roots will dry up.

HARVEST WILD FLOWER SEEDS

Generally I'm all in favour of perennials. They come back every year and they're not much hassle to grow. The only exceptions for me are wild flowers (most of which are annuals) to attract bees and other pollinators.

Wild flowers use the wind to sow their seeds but it can be a bit hit or miss. You can help them by harvesting seeds and sowing them yourself. Some seed pods are more obvious than others. You'll have noticed the bold heads of poppies; others take a bit more attention to spot.

You will need
- Plastic tubs for collecting in (free of holes)
- Paper towel
- Envelopes
- Pen for labelling

Store your seeds indoors, somewhere dry. If you only have space outside, pop the envelopes into a jar with a lid so that they can't get damp.

1 Walk round your own plot (and the gardens of others, if they're willing to let you look). You will need your eyes on full alert, looking for seed pods and heads.

2 To harvest the seeds, it's generally easier to take the whole seed head, as many seeds are too small to collect individually. Break off a head or two and put them in your tub. If you find several kinds, you might want to harvest them into separate tubs.

3 Leave the seeds to dry on a windowsill. When they're thoroughly dried out, you can put them into folded sheets of paper or in envelopes. Don't forget to label them.

Find more on harvesting other kinds of seeds on page 41.

daisies

Californian poppies

poppies

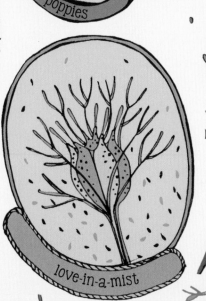

love-in-a-mist

CARVE A PUMPKIN

You've watered and tended your pumpkins and hopefully you've got a wonderful crop. They are ripe when they've turned a rich orange colour and the skin has hardened. You can use the whole pumpkin for cooking, or scoop out the flesh and carve it into a lantern.

You will need
- Pumpkin
- Sharp knife
- Metal spoon
- Small bowl
- Pen or pencil
- Blunter kitchen knife
- Tea light

Pumpkin skin can be very tough, so leave the sharp-knife action to the adults and get the kids to do everything else.

1 Use the sharp knife to carve a lid from the top of the pumpkin, cutting in a circle around the stem. When you're almost all the way around, cut a notch into the circle, so that it will be easy to replace the lid to a perfect fit.

2 Use the metal spoon to scoop out the flesh and seeds from inside (most people's favourite bit). Use the flesh for soup or pumpkin pie.

3 Separate out the seeds to wash and keep for next year. Leave them to soak in the small bowl while you are busy.

4 Once you've scooped out the insides, you'll be left with the thick pumpkin skin with a lid, all ready for carving. Either draw on your design with a pencil, or mark it out with the blade of the blunter kitchen knife.

5 Divide the work: a grown-up can carve into the outside skin along the design lines with the sharp knife, then a child can finish the gouging out from the inside of the pumpkin.

6 Once carved, put a tea light inside, light it, replace the lid and put the pumpkin on your porch or balcony.

BUILD A BUG HOUSE

Some insects die when autumn comes and the temperatures start to fall, but others look for a safe spot to overwinter before reappearing in spring. Help our wildlife good guys such as solo bees and ladybirds to stay in your garden by building them a bug house.

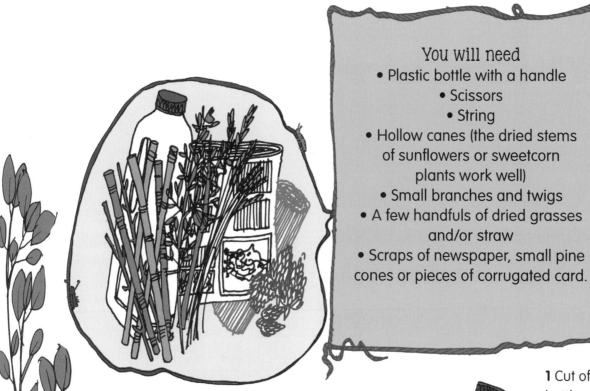

You will need
- Plastic bottle with a handle
- Scissors
- String
- Hollow canes (the dried stems of sunflowers or sweetcorn plants work well)
- Small branches and twigs
- A few handfuls of dried grasses and/or straw
- Scraps of newspaper, small pine cones or pieces of corrugated card.

1 Cut off the flat end of the plastic bottle with scissors, leaving the large end open.

2 Fill the bottle with your gathered materials, with some bits poking out of the bottle to help the bugs find their way in. The material should fit tightly in the bottle and not fall out.

3 Tie a string to the handle and hang the bug house up. So simple, anyone can do it!

A plastic milk or juice bottle with a handle can also make a scoop or mini shovel. Cut the end off at an angle and you have a neat, handy tool that kids will enjoy using.

MAKE AN AUTUMN WREATH

I've always preferred to make decorations rather than buy them - it's better for the environment. Here's a simple way to make a triangular autumn wreath without having to buy a lot of materials.

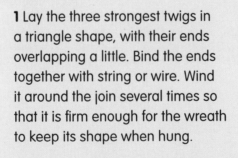

1

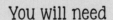

You will need
- Twigs and small branches
- Plenty of autumn foliage
(you can find this in your local park or woods as well as in the garden)
- String or thin wire
- Secateurs or strong scissors
- A length of colourful ribbon
(recycle old gift ribbon)

2

3

1 Lay the three strongest twigs in a triangle shape, with their ends overlapping a little. Bind the ends together with string or wire. Wind it around the join several times so that it is firm enough for the wreath to keep its shape when hung.

2 When you have a neat, strong twig triangle, use string or wire to add small twigs, autumn foliage and so on. Arrange them carefully as you attach them so that there is even coverage along the length of each side. Start at one joint and work your way around all sides.

3 Add your decorations, dried flowers or leaves and attach them on top. Finally, tie a loop of ribbon around the top joint of the wreath and hang it on your front door.

If you feel your wreath could be even more colourful, you could make some woollen pompoms in autumnal colours or add some additional ribbon bows.

You can also use your wreath to recycle small decorations or other bits and pieces from your craft drawer.

Winter

KEEP SEEDS FOR NEXT YEAR

Some of the fruit, vegetables and flowers that I've suggested you grow have an added benefit - they'll provide you with seeds for next year, so you won't need to buy more.

Peas, pumpkins, sweetcorn, nasturtiums and sunflowers all have seeds that are easy to harvest and can be stored in envelopes. Tomatoes, carrots and beetroot seeds are more difficult to harvest.

When buying seeds, look out for naturally pollinated or heirloom types. These are more likely to work when you harvest seed from the adult plants. They're preferable to bred hybrids (generally labelled as such), which tend to have seed that doesn't save so well, and is sometimes even sterile. If you've kept the packets, or know the variety names, label the envelopes they're stored in.

Sweetcorn
Leave a cob on the stalk to save for seed. When it has dried up, pick the cob and pull the leaves back from the kernels. Tie string around this and hang the cob up in a warm dry place. When it's dried out, rub the seeds off the cob.

Sunflowers
Cut the finished flower heads off and rub off the flossy substance that covers the seeds. Leave them to dry in a warm place. After a few weeks rub off the dried seeds.

Peas
Leave peas that you want to use for seeds on the plants until they've dried out. When they're ready, the peas will rattle in the dry, brown pods.

Nasturtiums
When the petals have dropped, leave the seed pods until they have dried up then take out the seeds, which look like chickpeas. Leave them to dry out in a warm place.

Pumpkins
When the pumpkin is dried out (the skin will be rock hard), then cut it into chunks and separate the seeds out from the flesh. Wash the sticky pulp off them, spread them out on paper in a warm place to dry, then store the largest, plumpest seeds.

MAKE A SUNFLOWER-HEAD BIRD FEEDER

Birds love sunflower seeds, and when your sunflowers are over, you can make a super-simple feeder from a flower head, to help keep the birds happy through the winter.

You will need
• Sunflower head
• String
• Sticky tape
• Short, strong piece of stick or metal skewer

1 When the flower petals have shrivelled and the head is covered with yellow fluff, cut the head off the stem, leaving about 10cm of stalk.

Hang the flower head inside to dry for at least a week or two (it will keep for as long as you want). When it is thoroughly dried out, rub the yellow fluff off the seeds.

Attach one end of a piece of string to one end of the stick or skewer with sticky tape. Make a hole up through the stem of the flower head into the back of the flower head, then out through the front of it.

2 Push the stick or skewer through the hole, pulling the string with it. Tie the end of the string around the stem several times to stop it pulling through. At the other end, make a loop to hang up the bird feeder.

3 Hang the feeder up outside, somewhere where you'll have a good view of the visiting birds. The face of the sunflower makes its own table: birds can land there and peck out the seeds. If you hang it out in midwinter, when food is scarce, the birds will love you for it!

The yellow fluff that dusts the flower face is actually made up of tiny 'extra' flowers which are called disc florets.

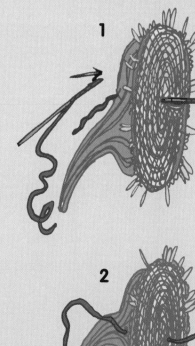

1

2

3

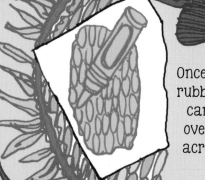

Once the fluff has been rubbed off the head, you can lay a piece of paper over it and rub a crayon across the seeds to see the patterns.

KEEP STEMS FOR NEXT YEAR'S CANES

When the sunflowers and corn have finished, and the ears of corn and flowers are gone, the plants still have something left to give! Here's an easy reuse tip.

You will need
- Sunflower or sweetcorn stems
- Sharp knife or pair of secateurs
- A dry place to store the stems, or a tarp to wrap them in to keep them dry if you need to store them outside

The stems of sunflowers and sweetcorn are really tough – so tough that they're strong enough to use as stakes and supports for next year's plants. You need to harvest them before they get wet, or they will start to rot.

1 Use the knife or secateurs to cut the stalks off at an angle very near the base.

2 Rip off any loose leaves, and cut off any side stems. Cut away any thin or flimsy parts at the top of the main stem.

3 Store the stems in a cool, dry place. Keeping them dry is crucial; they will rot if damp.

Once fully dried out and hard, these stems make great stakes for tomatoes or supports for climbing crops such as peas. And they're totally free!

HOW DO SEEDS GROW?

Here's a fascinating experiment that shows you what will be happening under the soil when you plant seeds and they start to grow. Watch the whole germination process indoors - you can try this at any time of year.

1 Soak the broad bean in a bowl of tepid water overnight.

2 Soak several sheets of paper towel in water, and fold them small enough to fit flat into the plastic bag. Slide in the wet paper towel so that it lays flat inside the bag.

3 Place the broad bean between the towel and the side of the bag, so that you can see it clearly. Gently flatten down the bag and seal it (to prevent moisture escaping).

4 Use tape to stick the bag to a window (the warmth of the light coming through the window will help the bean to germinate).

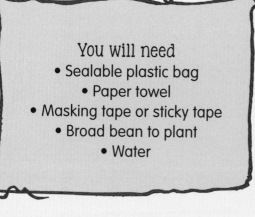

You will need
- Sealable plastic bag
- Paper towel
- Masking tape or sticky tape
- Broad bean to plant
- Water

5 Now you just wait! It may take a couple of weeks but the bean will sprout as it warms. You could get the children to draw the bean's outline on the outside of the bag every day to help them chart its progress.

Soon you should see the roots (the radicle) begin to grow downwards, and the first shoots (called the epicotyl) start to sprout out of the bean coating (known as the testa).

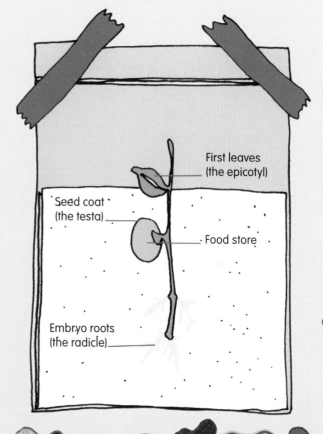

First leaves (the epicotyl)

Seed coat (the testa)

Food store

Embryo roots (the radicle)

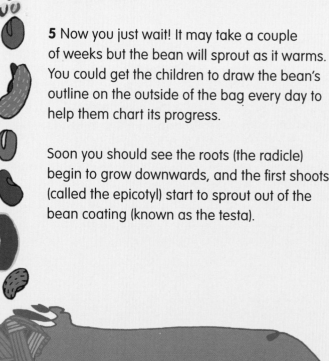

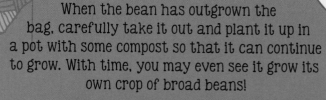

When the bean has outgrown the bag, carefully take it out and plant it up in a pot with some compost so that it can continue to grow. With time, you may even see it grow its own crop of broad beans!

FROST AND COLD-WEATHER GARDENING

Winter is an opportunity for gardeners to have a well-earned rest, but there are some jobs you can do to give yourself a head start in the spring. Here's how to protect your strawberry plants from frost and make mini greenhouses to protect seedlings from the cold.

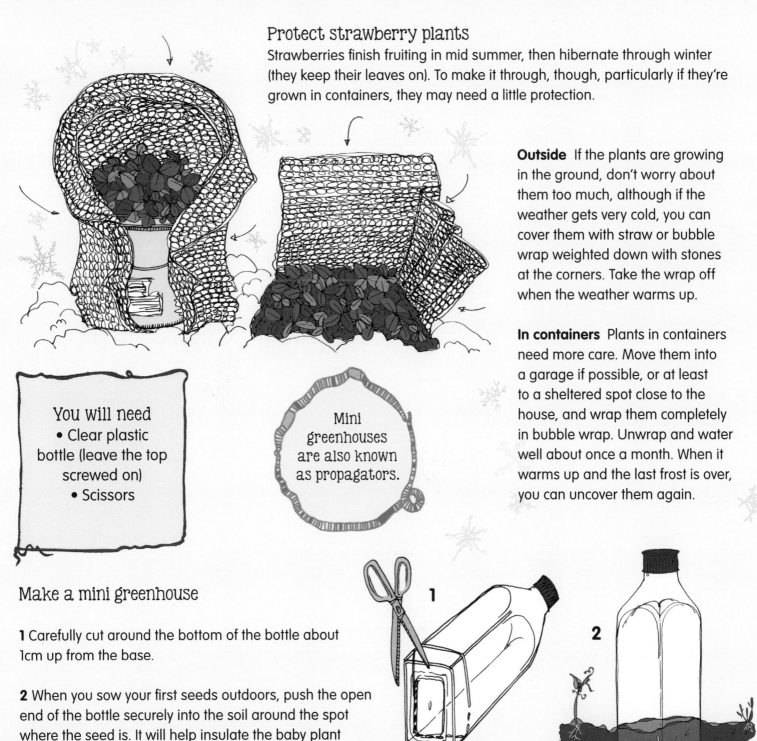

Protect strawberry plants

Strawberries finish fruiting in mid summer, then hibernate through winter (they keep their leaves on). To make it through, though, particularly if they're grown in containers, they may need a little protection.

Outside If the plants are growing in the ground, don't worry about them too much, although if the weather gets very cold, you can cover them with straw or bubble wrap weighted down with stones at the corners. Take the wrap off when the weather warms up.

In containers Plants in containers need more care. Move them into a garage if possible, or at least to a sheltered spot close to the house, and wrap them completely in bubble wrap. Unwrap and water well about once a month. When it warms up and the last frost is over, you can uncover them again.

You will need
• Clear plastic bottle (leave the top screwed on)
• Scissors

Mini greenhouses are also known as propagators.

Make a mini greenhouse

1 Carefully cut around the bottom of the bottle about 1cm up from the base.

2 When you sow your first seeds outdoors, push the open end of the bottle securely into the soil around the spot where the seed is. It will help insulate the baby plant against cold temperatures for the first few weeks of spring.

MAKE SEED BOMBS

Kids love making seed bombs - a great rainy-day activity. You can use up any extra seeds you have left over from your harvest and make some green (and economical) gifts, too. What's not to love?

You will need

- Clay (go for the standard type rather than air-drying clay)
- Compost
- Seeds (a good handful; wild flower seeds work best, but you can use any seeds you have left over from summer)
- Mixing bowl
- Spoon
- Water
- Baking tray or newspaper
- Small paper bags and crayons to decorate them

1 Take a handful of compost and a couple of spoonfuls of seeds and stir them together in a bowl. Mix in a handful of the clay, and knead together, adding a little water if the mix is too dry and stiff (aim for a dough-like consistency that's malleable but not sloppy).

2 Roll the mixture into little balls (seed bombs) around 2cm in diameter. When you've used up all the mixture, leave them to dry on some newspaper sheets in a cool, dry place (nowhere too warm or they may dry too quickly and split).

3 When the seed bombs are thoroughly dried out, pop a few in decorated paper bags ready to give as presents.

1

2

3

STRING POPCORN FOR DECORATIONS

We were making popcorn to eat in front of a movie, and the idea of stringing it into garlands came up. It was a hit: it's become a family tradition.

Strings of popcorn make a good addition to decorated trees, and using your own home-grown popping corn makes them extra special.

1 Cut a length of yarn about 2m, and tie a looped knot at one end. Thread a needle through the other end.

2 Thread the puffed kernels on to the needle one by one, and gently ease them on to the yarn. It will work best if the needle goes through the centre of the kernel, or at least through one of the bigger, puffy bits. The occasional piece will crumble and fall off.

3 If you're doing this with smaller children or as part of a larger group, cut shorter lengths of yarn. You can tie them together to make a longer string when everyone has finished their own piece.

You will need
- A big bowl of popped corn
- Ball of yarn
- Large, thick yarn needles, one per person, big enough for kids to handle easily

4 Some strings can have the popcorn spread thinly, with coloured yarn showing in the gaps, or bunch the kernels up close for a denser effect: either looks good.

5 When you've finished, drape the popcorn string around, stand back and admire!

ABOUT THE AUTHOR

Esther Coombs is a professional illustrator living and working in rural Kent, UK with her lovely husband and daughter (who's a fantastic tree climber). She is probably best known for her busy black-and-white line drawings, mostly in books and on large-scale public art (she loves a very big drawing!). Recent clients include: Hampshire Cultural Trust, Kyle Books UK, The Watts Gallery and commercial developers. She is also the illustrator of two children's activity books, *The New York Activity Book* and *The London Activity Book* (also published by Button Books), and is currently working on a children's story about a very special cake. The inspiration for *Plant, Sow, Make & Grow* came from running the gardening club at her daughter's school and a charming series of newsletters, which she produces and illustrates herself in the same informative and approachable style as this book. She encourages everyone to get outside and grow something you can eat!

esthercoombs.com, follow her on Instagram: @esthercoombsillustration

Show us your gardening projects with the hashtag #plantsowmakeandgrow

First published 2019 by Button Books, an imprint of Guild of Master Craftsman Publications Ltd, Castle Place, 166 High Street, Lewes, East Sussex, BN7 1XU. Text © Esther Coombs, 2019. Copyright in the Work © GMC Publications Ltd, 2019. Illustrations © Esther Coombs, 2019. ISBN 978 1 78708 024 9. All rights reserved. The right of Esther Coombs to be identified as the author of this work has been asserted in accordance with the Copyright, Designs and Patents Act 1988, sections 77 and 78. No part of this publication may be reproduced, stored in a retrieval system or transmitted in any form or by any means without the prior permission of the publisher and copyright owner. This book is sold subject to the condition that all designs are copyright and are not for commercial reproduction without the permission of the designer and copyright owner. While every effort has been made to obtain permission from the copyright holders for all material used in this book, the publishers will be pleased to hear from anyone who has not been appropriately acknowledged and to make the correction in future reprints. The publishers and author can accept no legal responsibility for any consequences arising from the application of information, advice or instructions given in this publication. A catalogue record for this book is available from the British Library. Publisher: Jonathan Bailey, Production: Jim Bulley, Jo Pallet, Commissioning Editor: Dominique Page, Senior Project Editor: Virginia Brehaut, Managing Art Editor: Gilda Pacitti. Colour origination by GMC Reprographics. Printed and bound in China.

For more on Button Books, contact:
GMC Publications Ltd, Castle Place,
166 High Street, Lewes, East Sussex,
BN7 1XU, United Kingdom
Tel: +44 (0)1273 488005
www.buttonbooks.co.uk